On This Day...

On This Day...
Notes from Above!

Linda Beverett
XULON PRESS ELITE

Xulon Press Elite
2301 Lucien Way #415
Maitland, FL 32751
407.339.4217
www.xulonpress.com

© 2020 by Linda Beverett

All rights reserved solely by the author. The author guarantees all contents are original and do not infringe upon the legal rights of any other person or work. No part of this book may be reproduced in any form without the permission of the author. The views expressed in this book are not necessarily those of the publisher.

Unless otherwise indicated, Scripture quotations taken from the King James Version (KJV) – *public domain.*

Scripture quotations taken from the Holy Bible, New International Version (NIV). Copyright © 1973, 1978, 1984, 2011 by Biblica, Inc.™. Used by permission. All rights reserved.

Paperback ISBN-13: 978-1-6312-9917-9

Ebook ISBN-13: 978-1-6312-9918-6

Dedication

*I*t is 1:27 am and I can't sleep. Sunday is Mother's Day, and my mother is in a nursing facility. I am so grateful that she is here with us, but if I'm honest, my heart hurts, and I know I am being selfish, but I wish she was "as she used to be."

I want her to anoint me with the olive oil that she has stocked up in her home that she has prayed over. And I want her to pray for me so that when I leave her presence, I feel better, although the situation is the same. I want her to tell me that *God* is in charge of everything and give my problems to him. I want the extra assurance that when I leave—and although she has prayed for me—she is still praying. I want her to call me because, somehow, she already knows that my heart is heavy, and she'll ask me, "Are you OK?" I say that I'm OK and she prays anyway. I want to be able to call her at 3:00 a.m., and just cry when I can't get the words out, and she'll pray until I stop crying! She has always known my heart and the pain I was going through internally, even though I never said a word! Years ago, she said, "Linda, you have been carrying a lot for a lot of years. It is time for you to give it all to *God*!"

Lord, I want to say *Thank you*, because as I am writing this, the tears have stopped and I feel myself smiling! I understand now, although she may not be "as she was," *I am blessed that she is still here.*

So now I will visit her and anoint her with oil and I will pray for her! I will ask her if she is OK and, even though she can't find the words to say, I will tell her to give it all to *God*, because He hears her *heart*! Everything that she did for me, *I will do for her*, which means, she is *still as she used to be!*

This book is dedicated to my mother. Thank you for the life you live as a Woman of God on purpose!
I love you, Mommy!

Table of Contents

Dedication v
A Journey of Growth and Sharing
through the Vehicle of Social Media ix
A Few Favorite Scriptures. xiii
In the Beginning—Seven Days xvii
31 Days Of Wisdom xxi

January's Journey
Hope and Faith 1
January's Relationship Reflections 5
Notes 7

February's Favor
Forgiveness 9
February's Relationship Reflections 13
Notes 15

March's Memoirs
Promise 17
March's Relationship Reflections 23
Notes 25

April's Accolades
Process and Progress 27
April's Relationship Reflections 31
Notes 33

May's Moments
Presence 35
May's Relationship Reflections 39
Notes 41

June's Jubilee
Love 43
June's Relationship Reflections 47
Notes 49

July's Jewels
Healing and Deliverance 51
July's Relationship Reflections 57
Notes 59

August's Aroma
Fear 61
August's Relationship Reflections 65
Notes 67

September's Sessions
Prayer 69
September's Relationship Reflections 73
Notes 75

October's Outlook
Doubt, Pain, Obedience, and Offense 77
October's Relationship Reflections 83
Notes 85

November's Nuggets
Encouragement 87
November's Relationship Reflections 93
Notes 95

December's Discussions
Trust 97
December's Relationship Reflections 103
Notes 105

A Journey of Growth and Sharing through the Vehicle of Social Media

A place where I can be connected while sitting in my living room. People that I haven't seen or heard from in years and even new people that I now get to call "friends" without touching them or hearing their voices. When I want a new dress and I can't or don't want to go to the store, no problem, just a few clicks and I have secured my new dress. When I need information on a particular subject and can't get to the library, no worries, I just Google it!

Since 2009, this has been a new part of my existence. The wonderful world of information and social media through the internet!!!

At first social media confused me because it was explained this way to me, "You can let people know where you are or what you are doing at any given time." But I thought, I don't think that I want folks to know where I am and certainly not what I am doing all of the time; that seemed way too personal!

However, as time passed and I began to navigate this new world of what seemed like utopia, I understood the context of the explanation more clearly. Everyone's experience on social media is different. In my experience, it has not solely been a means of receiving information, it has become so much more.

Every day is a new day and God provides His Word, enabling us through faith to reach His desired purpose and destiny for our lives. Through the power of God, social media has become a foreground for me to share wisdom gained through my life experiences anchored in the Word of God! It has been a vehicle used to transport words of affirmation and encouragement for the past eight years. A gift given in love, received in love, and now released back through love!

Proverbs 2:6—For the Lord gives wisdom; from his mouth come knowledge and understanding.

However, before this revelation, I wrestled with God over and over again! I said, "Why this, Lord? I don't know what I am doing, I don't know what to say. Who in the world am I to attempt to speak in authority on *anything* and what if I say the wrong thing? Lord, I don't want to say the wrong thing!"

Then I began to bargain with the Lord saying, "Why couldn't you give me the 'gift of song?' Everyone loves singers and there is no chance of me singing the wrong thing, Lord!" This was the essence of my chats with the Lord for a few years—all the while, continuing to *write*!

Then one day as I was writing, I *distinctly* heard God say, "The gift is not just for you." Wow, from that day going forward, I never questioned God again. That became the day that fear and doubt disappeared. I finally understood that although I am the writer, I am *not solely* the author and even though I may not always "get it right," I know that God has my back and He had it this entire time!

At the end of each chapter beginning with "January's Journey", there is a place that you too can jot down a few notes. I invite you to take this time to begin keeping a journal of what God is saying and showing you on a regular basis, so that the road map of your life becomes visible, knowing that He has traveled with you while navigating and directing you for your entire life!

So, as I have gathered my "memoirs," it is an extreme honor for me that you have chosen to travel this journey of "revisiting" with me, as I have placed on canvas what *God* has given me in this wonderful arena of social media through *words* of affirmation and encouragement, based on His Word!

My prayer is that something that is shared will touch your heart and bless you!

A Few Favorite Scriptures

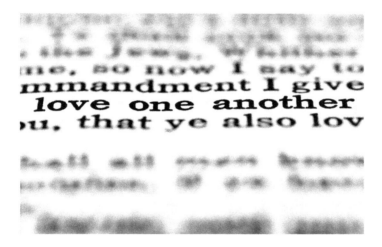

Proverbs 3:5–6
Trust in the LORD with all your heart and lean not on your own understanding; in all your ways submit to him, and he will make your paths straight.

Isaiah 41:10
Fear not, for I am with you; be not dismayed, for I am your God; I will strengthen you, I will help you, I will uphold you with my righteous right hand.

On This Day...

Psalms 37:4
Delight yourself in the LORD, and he will give you the desires of your heart.

Romans 3:23
For all have sinned, and come short of the glory of God.

Deuteronomy 31:6
Be strong and courageous. Do not be afraid or terrified because of them, for the LORD your God goes with you; he will never leave you nor forsake you.

2 Corinthians 5:7
For we walk by faith, not by sight.

1 Corinthians 13:4–8
Love is patient, love is kind. It does not envy, it does not boast, it is not proud. It does not dishonor others, it is not self-seeking, it is not easily angered, it keeps no record of wrongs. Love does not delight in evil but rejoices with the truth. It always protects, always trusts, always hopes, always perseveres. Love never fails. But where there are prophecies, they will cease; where there are tongues, they will be stilled; where there is knowledge, it will pass away.

A Few Favorite Scriptures

Proverbs 3-4
Let love and faithfulness never leave you;
bind them around your neck,
write them on the tablet of your heart.
Then you will win favor and a good name
in the sight of God and man.

Hebrews 11:6
But without faith it is impossible to please him: For he that cometh to God must believe that he is and that he is a rewarder of them that diligently seek him.

In the Beginning—Seven Days

***Genesis 1:4-5**—And God saw that the light was good, and He separated the light from the darkness. God called the light "day," and the darkness He called "night." And there was evening, and there was morning—the first day.*

<u>Sunday's Secrets</u>
Sundays are so easy to reflect on God and His magnificence, and many are taking the time to honor, magnify, worship, and praise Him by showing up to His house of prayer! I know that He is pleased because His Word says that He hears the prayers of the righteous! Sunday, the Lord's Day, is really no secret!

***Psalms 122:1**—I was glad when they said to me, "Let us go to the house of the* Lord.*"*

On This Day...

<u>Monday's Milestones</u>
We usually think of the "traditional" start of the workweek when we think of Mondays, and some may not be so excited about breaking the rest and relaxation of that oh, so needed two-day weekend. But even though some may remember the song "Rainy Days and Mondays" and feel a bit down and weary, being lovers of the Lord, it doesn't matter if it rains or shines on Mondays; the Son still shines strong!

2 Corinthians 4: 6—*For God, who said, "Light shall shine out of darkness," is the One who has shone in our hearts to give the light of the knowledge of the glory of God in the face of Christ.*

<u>Tuesday's Treasures</u>
Tuesdays are great because it is still the beginning of the week, and whatever your goals are, there is still plenty of time to accomplish them. God has been so patient with us, allowing time to meet us where we are and move us continuously toward His ever-lasting love!

John 17:3—*And this is life eternal, that they might know thee the only true God, and Jesus Christ, whom thou hast sent.*

<u>Wednesday's Wisdom</u>
Wednesdays are wonderful because we are now in the midst/middle of time within the week, and we have accomplished so much already! On Wednesdays, "hump day," we have gone too far to turn back. We have come to the height of our week while being invited to envision, be a part of, and move steadily toward the finish line!

Psalms 117:1-2—*Praise the* L<small>ORD</small>*, all you nations; extol him, all you peoples. For great is his love toward us and the faithfulness of the* L<small>ORD</small> *endures forever. Praise the* L<small>ORD</small>*.*

Thursday's Thoughts

Thursdays can sometimes be challenging because although it is the day before the last day of the workweek, there is still much to be accomplished, especially if the progress of the week has weaned. Thursday can at times be a press!

***Philippians 3:14**—I press toward the mark for the prize of the high calling of God in Christ Jesus.*

Friday's Focus

Thank God it's Friday. Not because it is the last workday of the workweek, but because God has graced us with continued purpose and progress to get to the end of a thing because the end is always better than the beginning! It is finished!

***Ecclesiastes 7:8**—The end of a thing is better than the beginning; the patient spirit is better than the proud in spirit.*

Saturday's Shout

Even as a child, Saturdays were always a joy because the week came to an end and obligations of home and school were met. We got to have fun without being on a schedule. We felt free!

***2 Corinthians 3:17**—Now the Lord is the Spirit, and where the Spirit of the Lord is, there is freedom.*

31 Days Of Wisdom

Proverbs 4:7—Wisdom is the principal thing; therefore, get wisdom: and in all thy getting get understanding.

- Day 1—Deviation and deflection can negatively affect the building blocks of character, which will put integrity at risk!

- Day 2—When we allow the Holy Spirit to be the author, Words become timeless!

- Day 3—Doing the same thing as someone else may still get different results. The act may look the same, but the essence of the act is the qualifier of the result!

On This Day...

- Day 4—Never desire anything or anybody more than you desire the presence and the righteousness of God; then, nothing can be dangled in front of you like a carrot!

- Day 5— If you don't know where you are going, any road will lead you there—-Bishop David G Evans, Facebook, 4/6/2018

- Day 6—Many opportunists are shapeshifters. Be slow about certain decisions and the change will be seen.

- Day 7—We are allowed to see it coming, but we can't stop it. The weather gives a constant reminder of *Who* is really in charge!

- Day 8—Many times we may fail in our endeavors; not because of talent or skill, but because of *ego*. Too smart for our own good! **Luke 14:11—For all those who exalt themselves will be humbled, and those who humble themselves will be exalted.**

- Day 9—There are times when it can be therapeutic to look back, because it shows just how far you have come, but don't go back!

- Day 10—Be careful who you drink and dine with, especially if you don't know the origin of the fountain. **1 Corinthians 10:31—So, whether you eat or drink, or whatever you do, do all to the glory of God.**

- Day 11—A seed will not grow even in fertile soil if it is not watered. Anything that is not fed will die.

- Day 12—A sacrifice is a seed; a sacrificial heart is the soil!

- Day 13—The quality of life in youth will usually reveal itself in maturity.

- Day 14—Hindsight is always clearer than the dim glass of foresight.

- Day 15—**Proverbs 22:1—A good name is to be more desired than great riches; favor is better than silver and gold.**

- Day 16—Great character is revealed in the way you treat someone who can do absolutely nothing for you and in doing something for someone who will never know that it came from you.

- Day 17—Integrity is much more precious than silver and gold!

- Day 18—There is no amount of money that can be paid in exchange of youth's sake because, too much would be at stake ...*wisdom!*

- Day 19—Prophets see the same thing everyone else does; they just "see" it differently— Bishop Mark Chironna, Twitter@ markchironna, 5/24/2018.

- Day 20—Looking back over the things that God has blessed me to write is like viewing a road map. It shows where I've been, how far I've come, and it is a great indication of where I am going! What road are you on?

- Day 21—**James 1:5—If any of you lacks wisdom, you should ask God, who gives generously to all without finding fault, and it will be given to you.**

- Day 22—Integrity and character charges us to take full responsibility for our actions.

- Day 23—What appears to some to be a daily mundane routine, is really a process for great promise! Keep praying, keep praising, keep working, keep speaking, keep singing, keep writing, etc. *Keep believing!*

- *Day 24*—Helping someone else heals you from what hurts you—-Bishop David G Evans, Facebook, 4/29/2018.

- Day 25—Some "love" you for what you do for them . . . until you can "do" no longer.

- Day 26—Lots of people want to ride in the limo with you, but what you want is someone who will take the bus with you when the limo breaks down. —Oprah Winfrey, https://www.brainyquote.com/quotes/oprah_winfrey_105255.

- Day 27—Character will only be revealed as the play unfolds.

- Day 28—When the enemy wants to conquer a man, he starts with his heart, not his head—-Bishop David G. Evans, Facebook, 4/20/2018.

- Day 29—The problem with dating integrity and good character is that those two don't usually show up on the first few dates. But be patient; they will either show up or stand you up. Take your time!

- Day 30—Favor does not create friends; it creates enemies and audits friendships—-Bishop David G. Evans, Twitter @davidgevans1, 11/28/2014.

- Day 31—Sometimes it is wise to say, "I don't know." Don't try to prove you know it all; you will end up disproving it the more you talk—-Bishop Mark Chironna, Twitter@markchironna, 3/16/2020.

January's Journey

Hope and Faith

Hebrews 11:1—Now faith is confidence in what we hope for and assurance about what we do not see.

- ❖ The enemy wants your waiting to descend from patience to complacency. But remember, Faith is active!
- ❖ Tight spaces can sometimes cause us to want to break out on our own, outside of faith.
- ❖ Faith puts your name on things that you cannot see—Bishop David G. Evans, Facebook, 12/2/2019.
- ❖ Sometimes we have to close our eyes to reason, and open our ears so that we can see! **Romans 10:17—So then faith comes by hearing, and hearing by the Word of God.**

- Faith is your God-given evidence that what you are hoping for is real.
- You will receive "what you say" by faith, good or bad. Be intentional with your words.
- When God is ready to bless you by faith, He will make "the enemy" handover everything that was held up or stolen.
- Anticipate and believe every good thing today, thereby overshadowing everything that the enemy attempts to send to rebut!
- Faith ushers us to promise.
- You can't get to the destination without taking the trip. Faith navigates the trip!
- Command your morning so that your day is revelatory by the strength and power of your faith.
- Whatever you have been asking God for, never stop asking Him! Although we see through a dim glass at times, especially concerning our future, that is OK. If it is in His will for you, if you thought it and envisioned it, then it exists. Keep on asking, seeking, and knocking!! *It is always too soon to quit!*
- Radical faith says, I will get all of the promises of God while staring the negative circumstances in the face.
- **Be blessed today, everyone!**
- Sometimes God leads and sometimes He guides, but know this: Wherever He is taking us, He has already gone ahead to prepare the way. **Exodus 13:21—By day, the LORD went ahead of them in a pillar of cloud to guide them on their way and by night, in a pillar of fire to give them light so that they could travel by day or night.**
- You will know when God has given you an assignment because no matter how much opposition, pain, suffering, or time that you have endured, abandonment will not be an option. *Faith reigns.*

- **Romans 1:17—For therein is the righteousness of God revealed from faith to faith: As it is written, the just shall live by faith.**

- Don't let "I'm waiting on God" become a cliché for you to wither away into nothingness. Faith without *action* is dead!

- Never get weary of doing the right thing, while others seem to be having the time of their life doing the "wrong thing." Eventually, they all have to come back home. So be joyful, happy, and grateful that you are the "sibling of the Prodigal Son!" Have faith in the Father. *Luke 15:31—"My son," the father said, "you are always with me, and everything I have is yours."*

- Faith is your heart's response to God's instruction—Bishop David G. Evans, Twitter@davidgevans1, 4/6/2018

- Those that were going to be blessed by Joseph's dream attempted to kill him. Sometimes even those that are close to you will not understand or agree with God's dream for you! Keep loving them and move forward anyway.

- Since God said it, believe it and receive it. It Is so!

- Whatever your "it" is, when "it" is ordained by God, and you have faith, "it" will come to pass; not because of you or me …But God!

- Because of the faith of Abraham, Sarah received the promise. When you have a God-given assignment with another person or persons, God will make sure it is received so that His purpose and promise come to pass, through faith.

- Never allow your faith to be negatively affected by someone else's action or opinion. Remember, there were two of everything in the Ark! **Matthew 24:12—And because iniquity shall abound, the love of many shall wax cold.**

- Know your worth and wait on the Lord with unwavering faith!

- There is no greater outcome than your God-given faith forged with His will …power!

- ❖ Hope is the crossroad to faith. It moves you closer; it gets to your destiny. Never give up hope.
- ❖ Faith acts like a thing is so, even when it's not so, that it might be so—Bishop David G. Evans, Facebook and sermons beginning 2011.
- ❖ Certain doors can close and re-open! Faith opens doors again.
- ❖ Sometimes we doubt God because of emotional clutter. Clear the clutter through renewed faith and reclaim His promises! **1 Corinthians 14:33—For God is not a God of confusion but of peace....**
- ❖ Faith is believing that one without the others is impossible . . . Father, Son, and Holy Spirit!

January's Relationship Reflections

★ Relationship did not begin with the union of our mothers and fathers. It began with a sovereign God. He created relationships on the sixth day with a man and a woman and He was pleased. We did not choose God, He chose us; so rest in the truth that you and I are Chosen! We are in relationships with each other, because of our relationship with God first! This is the *ultimate relationship*! **1 John 4:19—We love because he first loved us.**

★ Evaluate a prospective interest by the "content of his or her character," not the age on their birth certificate.

- Remember that a God connection is two people walking together in the same accord, but it may not happen *instantaneously*, all at one time or in a projected timeframe. Walking together can take many twists and turns before the "same accord" completely manifests. Be patient with each other!

- The body of Christ is made up of many parts to make a whole and so it is with relationships. All of one is required, as well as all of the other, to make up the *whole*! That is a simple application, right? Then why is the process so complicated for many? Don't let ego get in the way of one, the other, both, or all! **1 Corinthians 12:12—There is one body, but it has many parts. But all its many parts make up one body. It is the same with Christ.**

- God will keep us hidden in plain sight so that His future connection is preserved for us. Trust His plan for your life!

Notes

February's Favor

Forgiveness

1 John 1:9—If we confess our sins, he is faithful and just to forgive us our sins and to cleanse us from all unrighteousness.

- ❖ Forgiveness frees us to receive God's blessings.
- ❖ We have to fight the enemy every day of our lives, so let us not be so hard on one another.
- ❖ The door to promise can't be accessed without forgiving *first*!
- ❖ Pray for those who hate or dislike you. They need a breakthrough by way of your prayer.

- Do the right thing even when you know someone who you *think* does not deserve it, will benefit.

- When you forgive someone today and tomorrow those old feelings creep up again toward the same person, then just forgive again until your heart becomes new, along with a transformed mind. So, stop beating yourself up. Let Jesus' help work it out of you. *Forgive again*!

- When you repent from sin you are forgiven by God, and He graces you to be able to bear the consequences of those actions!

- Guilt was never meant to be a place to occupy. It is a doorway to repentance and liberty! There is no condemnation in God!

- Respect is almost impossible to regain once it has been completely torn away . . . But God!

- Transformation of the mind is a continuous work in process!

- Sometimes the best medicine for guilt is simply a direct, heartfelt apology. It frees the bound!

- When we so readily see a flaw in someone else, it may be that we are deflecting. God has a magnificent way of revealing us to ourselves!

- Indifference is not strength: It is a coping mechanism that can ultimately separate you from God.

- **Happy Valentine's Day!**

- We have to forgive each other, our inheritance rests on it.

- The twenty-four-hour rule: If someone has gotten on your nerves with a comment or action, if possible, wait twenty-four hours before you respond. This does not mean that you hold on to anger. It means that the opposite should happen, and many times you will find that there is no need for a response. Don't allow the outburst of other people's emotions to control you! Time will give you clarity, and you will be less likely to lead with your emotions. It matures you and it works!

- ❖ Don't allow anything or anyone to cause you to become bitter. Bitterness disconnects you from God. Choose to forgive so that you can move past the hurt while staying secure in God's arms!

- ❖ Don't allow the past, people, and most importantly, ourselves, to immobilize us into a state of guilt. All things are necessary pieces to complete the puzzle. It had to happen! Our responsibility is to learn all that we can from every piece so that we can move into the next dimension of our lives.

- ❖ Unforgiveness is not a respecter of persons. It is transferable to anyone who is a reflection of the offender to the offended.

- ❖ And the Lord restored the fortunes of Job when he prayed for his friends. Forgive them and pray for them. It is time for double! **Job 42:10—After Job had prayed for his friends, the Lord restored his fortunes and gave him twice as much as he had before.**

- ❖ God knows, He already searched your heart. Forgive yourself.

- ❖ Unforgiveness is a secret internal weapon that can hide for decades. It destroys anyone who houses it. Forgive and take your life back.

- ❖ While we don't know what Jesus wrote in the sand, I believe that every accuser there *saw exactly* what He wrote concerning their individual sinful lives. The *same* shame, guilt, and accusations that they attempted to bring against the woman caused each one of them to slip or sneak away one by one, starting with the one who lived the longest, until there were no more! We all have planks in our eyes that need to be *continuously* seen and removed through repentance! **John 8:1–12.**

- ❖ When you realize that someone does not care for you or dislikes you, did you wrong, or even deemed themselves to be your enemy, once you get over the hurt feelings or the "I don't care attitude" or even attempting to *make* them change their mind (which, by the way, is impossible) . . . *forgive them*. Then, pray for them and watch God work in their life. That, my brothers and sisters, is an example of turning the other cheek ... yours and theirs!

- ❖ A few days ago, my heart was heavy, wondering if dislike and negative opinions would continue to keep me in "lock-up" forever, even though I have lived in repentance for years. But late in the midnight hour, *light walked in*! I couldn't help but shed tears because *God* said—I *alone* have released the chains and taken you *out of time-out a long time ago. I got you*! That is *the power of God*!

- ❖ Repentance must come after sin so that there is freedom.

- ❖ David was not the "apple of God's eye" because he was perfect, but because he was *repentant* in his heart!

- ❖ It is one thing to hurt someone unintentionally, but it is completely different to plan someone's pain! Seek God's forgiveness ... first!

- ❖ Forgiveness can be a continuous process. Ask for *God's* help: He answers prayers!

February's Relationship Reflections

- ★ The Book of Ruth is a wonderful book and one of the only two Books in the Bible that is named after a woman. This means to me that God's magnificence is always more than "surface deep." While it tells a beautiful love story through a man and a woman, it is so much more than that! It is a story of redemption! Boaz is the keeper of the House of Bread. He is a type of Christ who allows us to come willingly to his field to "glean," to be fed and to be redeemed by God!—**The Book of Ruth**.

- ★ In the body of Christ, diversity brings unity. We have more in common than our differences—Bishop David G. Evans, Facebook, 4/29/2019.

- He may be quiet and reserved, yet not silent. He may also be caring, gentle, humble, disciplined, and determined in the relationship, all while being confident enough to *appear* to others as being inconspicuously strong and courageous... *until the storms hit!* He deserves respect and honor! Ignore outside distractions!

- Opposites attract—The very popular saying "opposites attract" is true, but maybe not in the context that many believe. Because if we are opposite of someone from the "core," even though there may be an initial attraction, there cannot be real cohesion or connection.

  Amos 3:3—How can two walk together, except they agree.

  Opinions vary and disagreements arise, but because we "walk together," by the end of the day, resolve should override differences because of the "core" connection. It may sound unrealistic to say "by the end of the day," but that has to be a working goal going in, starting over, starting now, and from now on! Also, it is biblical... **Ephesians 4:26—In your anger, do not sin; do not let the sun go down while you are still angry.**

  Furthermore, when one is feeling down, depressed, anxious, unworthy, hurt, sick, etc., those feelings which are housed in the frontal lobes will evoke the connection so that the encouraging/opposite side moves in to help facilitate healing. When both are feeling positive, the reserve is fueled, so that when both are in a negative place at the same time, the reserve kicks in from the third cord (or core) and begins to release healing so that the "state of the union" has re-connection without real interruption!

  So yes, opposites do attract, so that what each *committed* connection needs outside of themselves can be provided. *Pray together; it fuels the reserve!*

- Most relationships fail when one person takes hope from the other—Bishop David G. Evans, Facebook, 4/19/2018.

Notes

March's Memoirs

Promise

Luke 1:37—For no word from God will ever fail."

❖ Just because your timing was off, does not mean the promise is nullified! God is not an Indian giver!

❖ When they scrutinize your blessing but haven't seen your burdens, just say "I have been anointed for this."

❖ The problem with doing certain things in your own human effort is this: You are bound to keep that effort up until it fails and it will fail. However, when you have God's stamp of approval or favor of certain situations or people etched in His hand for your life, *it can't fail.*

- ❖ We will not feel wonderful, courageous, and encouraged all of the time; I know I don't. However, in those challenging times, we have to be still by doing what God says in His Word until help arrives, in the Spirit.

- ❖ If there is something that you want, no matter how bad you want it, if it does not line up with God's Word, then that desire did not come from God. He will never contradict His Word. Stay in the mind of God! **2 Corinthians 1:20—For all the promises of God in him are yea, and in him Amen unto the glory of God by us!**

- ❖ In this life, there will be times that you will go through a season or "be a season." For everything, there is a season. **Ecclesiastes 3:1—To everything there is a season, and a time to every purpose under the heaven.**

- ❖ When God reveals His promises to you and you "believe," expect the enemy's diversion. It illuminates and verifies the promises!

- ❖ When God makes a promise, He keeps it. Glorify Him for that!

- ❖ God's gifts are given freely; they cannot be earned.

- ❖ We will never find true answers outside of God!

- ❖ Just because it didn't happen yet, does not mean that God didn't say it. Stay or get back in destiny's lane and continue to be blessed.

- ❖ Whatever God allows, good or not so good, there is *always* a lesson in it! He is a wonderful Father and teacher!

- ❖ Stop missing God. Seek Him first and what He promised will find you. **Matthew 6:33—But seek ye first the kingdom of God, and his righteousness; and all these things shall be added unto you.**

- ❖ You are going to receive the promises by faith because they are not your promises—they are God's promises to you.

❖ Frustration of delayed promises is not unbelief, it actually reveals that we believe God's Word. Keep believing; *it shall come to pass*!

❖ God can restore something in your grandchild's life that was stolen or broken in yours.

❖ Ignore negativity's sidebars and keep walking until you walk right into promise!

❖ I was sitting here thinking about the Lord. I love Him so much because He knows how to "throw shade." He protects what belongs to Him. Don't mess with His Chosen, unless He gives permission, and even then, you better know the limits! *God's covenant can't be broken or changed*!

God shut down the entire kingdom of Abimelech, the King of Gerar! None of the women in the kingdom were able to conceive. No babies mean no future! God told Abimelech in a dream that he was a dead man because Sarah was another man's wife. He said, "If you touch her, I will kill you and everything that is connected to you." Whew!

God had a covenant with Abraham and nothing would stand in the way of His promise.

When God speaks a future over your life, He will bring kings to their knees if necessary. *His promise for your life will come to pass!* **Genesis 20.**

❖ Stop giving people power over your life, because many have no control over their own lives. The blind can give no direction to the blind! Sight and power come from God!

❖ **Trust God!**

❖ God's dream for you: When God gives you a dream, it is a glimpse of your future and that of others. It will take time to come to pass. Be very careful with whom you share your dreams; dream killers do exist. Submit to the process to get to the finished promise. Stay encouraged and stay close to God during the process. Dreaming a dream is *not just about you*. Finally, never close your eyes to a dream *or* give up what God has shown and promised! Reflect on the life of Joseph in the Bible. **Genesis: 37:1-10**

- God never forgot about you. He held on to you so that you could receive His best, according to His plan and purpose.

- Remember, God's gifts can't be earned; they are given freely through His grace and love for us. That's the kind of God we serve. He's just good like that!

- **Matthew 18:19—Again I say unto you, that if two of you shall agree on earth as touching anything that they shall ask, it shall be done for them of my Father who is in heaven.**

- God fulfilled His promise to Sarah at age 90, and she died at the age of 127, the only woman whose age at death is mentioned in the Bible. God is letting you know that your age doesn't matter. His promise for your life is what matters, and it will be fulfilled, and He will also give you time to enjoy it!

- Everything He wrote and everything He spoke belongs to you—-Bishop David G. Evans, Facebook, 1/15/2019

- If you lost yourself, but found something else, then you are still lost! But God sweeps the house until He finds His treasure . . . *you!* **Luke 15:8-10—Or suppose a woman has ten silver coins and loses one. Doesn't she light a lamp, sweep the house and search carefully until she finds it? And when she finds it, she calls her friends and neighbors together and says, "Rejoice with me; I have found my lost coin." In the same way, I tell you, there is rejoicing in the presence of the angels of God over one sinner who repents.**

- The dream was given to Pharaoh in two forms because the matter had been firmly decided by God, and *He* will do it soon! **Genesis 41:32—And for that, the dream was doubled unto Pharaoh twice; it is because the thing is established by God, and God will shortly bring it to pass.**

- You will recover because God knows the plans that He has for you.

- ❖ Joseph had many distractions on his way to the palace, but because his destiny was fixed by God, he made it every step of the way through process to destiny. Distraction may stop a dream, but it will not stop you if you have dreamed a dream, because it originates from God! **Genesis 37:9— And he dreamed yet another dream, and told it his brethren, and said, Behold, I have dreamed a dream more; and, behold, the sun and the moon and the eleven stars made obeisance to me.**

- ❖ Every scheme and plan from the enemy that threw you in multiple pits to die, failed miserably because you are still here and you are not bitter. You are better than ever because of the power of God in your life.

- ❖ Your life is not measured by a yardstick fabricated by "people," but the "Genuine DNA" that comes from God!

March's Relationship Reflections

- ★ Men: Because you are made in His image, you are powerful and therefore you will attract many women. But be careful that you choose the right woman. Remember, she will be an image-bearer as well! The right woman's treasures are revealed from the inside out. She will be familiar to you! You will know her *because* she knows God! **Proverbs 18:22—He who finds a wife finds what is good and receives favor from the LORD.**

- ★ Men don't look vulnerable, but the heart of a man is very sensitive—Bishop David G. Evans, Facebook, 4/19/2018.

- When you have someone entering into your life, loving you while noticing all of the bags that you brought with you and begins to help you unpack even the ones that you didn't know or remember that you had... that's a keeper! **Philippian's 2:4— Let each of you look out not only for his own interests but also for the interests of others.**

- Young Women: Never latch on to a man that causes you to live "underground." God will *never* send someone in your life that belongs to someone else. It doesn't matter how fine or handsome he is, where he takes you (at night or far away from the neighborhood), how "nice" he treats you, or what he buys you! It is all a mirage and will cause you to lose who God has made you to be. It may take years to discover or recover yourself again! Love yourself enough to *wait*!

- Young Women: Don't ignore "red flags." When you are initially meeting and attempting to get to know him, be aware of negative *actions* in conversations. For example, if you kindly disagree with something that he says or asks and if he is even *slightly* abusive in his verbal response, then look past that handsome face, big house, beautiful car, etc., so that you can see the *bright red flag!*

Notes

April's Accolades

Process and Progress

Philippians 1:6—For I am confident of this very thing, that He who began a good work in you, will perfect it until the day of Christ Jesus.

- ❖ God determined what the end would be, from the beginning. Absolutely *nothing* happens in the heavens or here on Earth, unless it is allowed by the All-Mighty!

- ❖ We can get so entangled with what we think we want and need that we become completely blinded to God's perfect will for our lives.

- ❖ If you want to really know someone, just keep watching and the veil will lift completely.

- Sometimes when we try and fix our problems without God, everything goes haywire.

- Don't make permanent decisions based on temporary conditions. It is only a storm!

- It happened, it was awful, and it hurt. Now, let's wipe our tears and put one foot in front of the other and keep moving toward God!

- God will meet you where you are so that He can lead and sometimes even push you out to where you need to be, but *He will never leave you*!

- When we are led and guided by the Word of God and Holy Spirit, we have the authority and God-given birthright because of Calvary to go out and evangelize simply through the life that we live as Christians. Let your light shine!

- We have to learn to recognize boundaries. If we are given a line that is spoken or even implied that should not be crossed, then don't cross it. If you make a mistake, then cross back over. It will stop confusion and hurt feelings. Instead, discern where there is access. There is always access!

- It is not always easy doing what God tells us, especially when we know that being obedient may very well get us the opposite of what we presently desire!

- See it, learn it, and then move past it!

- **There is relief in the air today—praise God**

- Healing and deliverance are "tucked away" in *process*.

- When we keep walking by and *purposely* refrain from connecting, then—guess what?—there is an invader/intruder on the inside . . . an internal infection!

- Authentic. Words *and* Actions must match. If not, then we may be harboring a counterfeit! We all need a full-length *mirror*!

Process And Progress

- God's blessing is in the breaking and the crushing.
- Precisely timed calculated moves may boost your popularity with people, but it does nothing to seat you at the right hand of God!
- The greater the challenge, the greater the blessing!
- When experience screams *give up*, hope whispers *try again*. Listen for that still, small voice.
- Through foresight, we can see the beginning or the end; through hindsight, we see the significance.
- Reject every negative seed today, making room for the soil to produce blessings only!
- Sometimes we have to go back to the drawing board and start all over again. Seek His face, that is where the *revelation* is!
- We can have seasons in our lives when we are so weighed down that we don't notice because it has become our "normal"; but when the weight lifts, we can't help but praise God for the lifting and keeping us in spite of all of that pressure!
- "Giving" should come from the heart to the heart; any other route taken is just a transaction.
- It took almost a lifetime to appreciate and be grateful for God's no's. It's His protection!
- Recipe to maintain Godly Hope and Healing:
    1. Wake up and chat with God, *Pray*.
    2. Pick two scriptures and meditate on both.
    3. Be intentional about staying close to your house of prayer.
    4. Continuously tell and show your family and friends that you love them.
    5. Eat healthy meals, they keep your temple strong.
    6. Move your temple; get some form of exercise on a regular basis.

7. Most important, glorify and praise God in all of the above.

❖ Being honest about your life/testimony is a gift that you give for someone else to unwrap!

❖ No matter how "dirty" something gets, it can always be cleaned up. That also includes all of us. God works well with dirt!

❖ Man makes plans and God plans, but God is the best of planners!

❖ Difficult tasks and responsibilities become bearable, doable, and are even lifted, when the load is shared in the power of the Holy Spirit!

❖ What you should and shouldn't have is usually in close proximity together .... on purpose. Choose wisely!

April's Relationship Reflections

★ We will not agree on everything and yes there are "deal breakers." This is determined by the standards that *you* set, based on who you know you are in God. Furthermore, when the deal is broken, it should be broken in love . . . godly love.

★ If you feel that you have to "dumb down" for the sake of having a particular man or woman in your life, then that may not be the right person for you. The right person will recognize, require, and need all of who you are now and all you will become in God.

★ There is no prerequisite to love, but *trust must be earned!*

- ★ If you are considering spending your life with someone and you are not sure, then you need to ask yourself a question. Most times the question is not "Do I love this person?" because that will more than likely be yes, but ask yourself "Do I trust this person?" If the answer is anywhere near a maybe or no, then you may want to rethink your consideration.

- ★ Agape allows you to open your heart to *all*, Philo moves you to extend your heart to a selected few, and Eros drives you to give your heart to *one*!

Notes

May's Moments

Presence

Jeremiah 29:13—You will seek me and find me when you seek me with all your heart.

- ❖ Words are so beautiful, but they have a tendency to be misunderstood especially when presence is lacking.
- ❖ You know you have a special relationship with God when He begins to share His secrets with you for *your* life.
- ❖ God's presence will keep us in His lane for our lives, even when we are tempted to change. He is our internal GPS.
- ❖ Know your Father's voice. He will never tell you anything that goes against His Word.

- God does not change; He simply filled you yesterday for your soul's purpose of tomorrow. Purpose and destiny must be revealed!
- It takes moments to think *one wrong thought* that moves to one wrong word, then to one wrong action, which then regenerates itself outside of the original soil from which it came, and it takes lifetimes to die!

Think about this:

Philippians 4:8

Finally, brethren, whatsoever things are true, whatsoever things are honest, whatsoever things are just, whatsoever things are pure, whatsoever things are lovely, whatsoever things are of good report; if there be any virtue, and if there be any praise, think on these things.

- **Joshua 1:9—Have I not commanded you? Be strong and courageous. Do not be afraid; do not be discouraged, for the Lord your God will be with you wherever you go.**
- When we take up residence in the secret place of God's presence, we have given the enemy permission to wear himself out!
- The secret place is not just a place of protection, but it is a place of revelation.
- You can be "around" someone for years and not *know* them. Presence has to be revealed!
- Sometimes the strongest-looking can be the most fragile.
  - **I prayed for all of us this morning.**
- It doesn't matter what someone says to or about you that may be negative, but what really matters is *your perception* of what is said! You get to choose the outcome and how it will affect your life. Remember that you and the power of God are in charge! Learn how to release some stuff!

- Happiness is a by-product of joy. Joy originates from the Lord.

- When we dismiss what we don't understand, the blessing goes right along with the dismissal. Seek God, there is much that we don't understand!

- Everyone that speaks should *not* influence your direction. Be still so that you can discern! Sheep know the voice of their shepherd and follow. Know who is talking to you before you make a move!

- Even when our world within can take us to very low points because of life and circumstances and we feel disconnected and alone, we have to know that God never leaves us or forsakes us. When we *focus* on that reality, then our thoughts will begin to regenerate so that our world will change . . . within! God is our present help!

- If you don't know *who you are in God*, then you will *always* accept someone else's version of who they think you should be!

- What you think—positively or negatively—will seep into your heart and become *who you are*!

- Guard your heart by choosing the thoughts that will take up permanent residence!

- Doing the right thing for the wrong reason is still wrong. Renew your mind!

- Although it already exists, anything of true value is often challenging to discover!

- In times like these, when there are so many conflicting voices, we have to stay close to the Lord and those that He has assigned to lead us!

- Your heart can be a lonely place if you don't *really* share the contents. Enlarge your heart through God's presence.

- Divine connection is an assurance that the connection is always present, even when you are not in close proximity.

- There was an exchange at the Cross. Jesus took the sin and we took on the righteousness of God—Bishop David G. Evans, Facebook, 7/12/2017.

- When we strive for a closer relationship with the Lord, He will move us out of the dark into His light!!

- The "fat or fullness" of God's anointing will destroy every negative seed that continues to seasonally reproduce in your life!

- God is not a respecter of persons. He shines His sun on all.

- Daytime intimacy with GOD leads to nighttime conversations (dreams)—-Bishop David G Evans, Facebook, 10/23/2017.

- I want to take this time to *glorify* and *honor* the Lord this morning because five years ago, I spent ten days in the hospital undergoing an unanticipated and unplanned major operation! I thank you, Father, for holding on to me, for keeping me and for preserving my life. I promised you then and that promise continues; I will strive to do your will, a*ll the days of my life*! It is in the mighty matchless name of Jesus that I pray—Amen!!!

May's Relationship Reflections

Reflection

- ★ Many times, the one who loves and adores you is not saying words to hurt you; they may be saying words that may have hurt *them* in the past, which may be a deflection! Both of you mirror each other in many ways! Everyone has a history. There is no getting around it; bags have to be unpacked! You have to trust that God has sent you the right one so that you can unpack together!

- ★ Be very careful who you share with when you are upset and have problems with your love relationship. When you resolve your issue with them, the folks that you shared with may still be upset with the one that you *love*! If you have to consult someone to mediate issues in your relationship, then pastors, therapists, and counselors may be great choices because they are called to hear from God or trained professionals to help you navigate through your issues. Just as important, you get to keep the integrity and sanctity of your relationship without the biased opinions of others.

★ Never take those that love and care about you for granted . . . even God has a limit!

★ When a man or woman that you have known in the past suddenly becomes attracted to you after your accomplishments, be very careful of the place that you set for them at your table!!

★ Negative past relationships should not make us cynical and untrusting, but we should become a bit wiser so that we are able to share *wisdom*!

Notes

June's Jubilee

Love

1 John 4:8—Anyone who does not love does not know God, because God is love.

- ❖ A single word or act of love can break the barrier of hate or even indifference.
- ❖ **1 John 4:16—And so we know and rely on the love God has for us. God is love. Whoever lives in love lives in God, and God in them.**
- ❖ If you want to see what you are really dealing with in your daily life, it can only be viewed through *love*! All other feelings (hate, envy, fear, doubt, etc.) are blinders!

- *Love* will cause what is good on the inside to *spontaneously* breakthrough to the outside.

- God will test your limits so that you will realize that with Him, through love, your borders have expanded!

- If we are challenged with receiving love, then we will be challenged with giving love. We have to learn to be open to receive. Remember, God loved us *first*!

- Before we knew God, He loved us. When we discover His love for us, we develop a strong desire to give Him our all. True love is interactive!

- One moment we are weak; the next we feel strong. Thank God that love stands in the gap.

- When there is a divine connection, the ability to please is almost effortless because the desire stems from familiar hearts.

- Love by example. It is the gift that God has given us to overcome the *En-e-me*!

- Let's each do something good for someone today. I already have my someone in mind … who is yours?

- Our Love for God is the unveiling of His presence in our lives; it is His response—because *He loved us first*!

- In the midst of all of the hate and violence, let us turn that around in our own space by showing care, concern, and *love* for those in our hemispheres!

- We have to remember and know that against all odds and in the midst of everything that wants to block, hinder, delay—or stop—our process and progress, it will not prosper because love is still the way!

- Unconditional love—God says, no matter what, my grace is sufficient and *My love never fails*!

- God has given us the gift of love, and while this does not exonerate us from responsibility, it allows us to be forgiving, charitable, and tender to each other's faults, mistakes, and inconsistencies. Love covers a multitude of sins and is the vehicle that allows us to ultimately see each other as God does. **1 Peter 4:8—Above all, love each other deeply, because love covers over a multitude of sins.**

- Love does not exist to be sanctioned or controlled, but it is a wonderful gift from God that is given freely!

- Many people are not really afraid of giving love. They are afraid of either not receiving or receiving and losing love. Open your heart. God loves *you*!

- The kinsman next in line to purchase Elimelech's property did not want to claim it because Ruth, who was a Moabite, gentile, and sinner, was part of that redemption, and he thought that would ruin his estate and reputation. As a result of his predetermined prejudice, Boaz gained the ability to redeem Elimelech's property, which included Ruth, a redemption that was of great value to him. Others may not want us because of our past or background, but God loves and wants us because He sees in us who He has already called us to be! **Ruth 4:5–6—Then Boaz said, "On the day you buy the land from Naomi, you also acquire Ruth the Moabite, the dead man's widow, in order to maintain the name of the dead with his property." At this, the guardian-redeemer said, "Then I cannot redeem it because I might endanger my own estate. You redeem it yourself. I cannot do it."**

- Have you ever known someone who knew exactly what food you like, where you like to go, what you like to do? And they somehow provided it most of the time? And you thought that this person is wonderful because you wondered how they knew all of this? Well, that is because they loved you enough to "Pay attention!" That is just a small example of the Lord's love for you. He knows you well enough to provide all you could ever ask or need!

- I have decided to stick with love. Hate is too great of a burden to bear—Dr. Martin Luther King Jr., **https://www.brainyquote.com/quotes/martin_luther_king_jr_297520**

- ❖ This is what love can do: The presence of hate can be felt like a fiery furnace, but loving God and being obedient in the midst of haters and enemies will move God to *put the flames out!* Shadrach, Meshach, and Abednego were not burned! **Daniel 3:8–28—The Fiery Furnace.**

- ❖ Be patient with family members, friends, love ones, co-workers, etc.; it takes some a bit longer to recognize and accept *agape (Love)*!

- ❖ Your heart is the treasure in your chest that gives you access to God and others!

- ❖ **Walls have recorded history. Saturate your home with the power of prayer!**

- ❖ Love provides a safe haven for different views and opinions to be expressed and accepted without diminishing a relationship. Acceptance does not always mean agreement! Love covers!

- ❖ *God's* love is so persistent that He keeps opening a door, anticipating His Son's arrival. He wants us, His firstborn, back (Adam). He is waiting!

- ❖ You will know when it is time to "let go" because what you have covered, nurtured, and held on to begins to fly on its own!

- ❖ Communication is a gift. Tell someone that you love them today!

- ❖ The moment we realize that we are not only loved by God, but He has poured His love into us, self-loathing and self-hate go right out of the window. We are no longer longing for "something" that we thought we needed . . . *We already have it!* Healing begins when love is released through receipt.

- ❖ The right kind of love will cause you to be still, then be led (guided) . . . willingly!

June's Relationship Reflections

- ★ Young women: A man who keeps his word is like finding precious buried treasure.

- ★ If you have been secretly harboring the Sarah "syndrome" in your heart, dismiss it from this moment forward. You are not too old to receive the blessings from God. As a matter of fact, you are the perfect age and this is your time! This is for all of the Abrahams as well!

- ★ Esther had no idea that she would be used by God to save a nation. God knows who and what you need to move you through to destiny. Be obedient to God's instructions by allowing Him to "arrange the marriage", so to speak, so that purpose and destiny will be fulfilled. —**The Book of Esther.**

★ We need to see every bit of God's magnificence, power, and glory, but we can't see it all if either or both of us are hiding! "It takes two to know *one*!"— **Gregory Bateson. AZQuotes.com, Wind and Fly LTD, 2020.**

https://www.azquotes.com/quote/906376, accessed June 15, 2020.

★ **Trivia**—Can you have a once in a lifetime love . . . twice in a lifetime?

Notes

July's Jewels

Healing and Deliverance

Jeremiah 17:14—Heal me, O Lord, and I shall be healed; save me, and I shall be saved, for you are my praise.

- ❖ Sometimes, letting tears flow is being strong.

- ❖ While some veils are meant to obscure or hide evil, some hide fear and weakness. But one thing is for sure: Once the veil is lifted, healing can begin!

- ❖ Freedom requires that we crave the desire of deliverance more than the comfort that the bondage has provided.

- Repentance is evidence of humility.

- Deliverance will never happen when standing on the outside looking in!

- Metastatic pathology is when a pathology/disease moves from the area of origin to different or secondary sites over time. We may think we are healed in one area because time has passed, but with no deliverance, the pathology just spreads to other areas in our lives.

- What is broken can usually be fixed, but it is impossible to fix what is "missing." Seek God!

- The problem you are facing is much smaller than our God!

- Did you know that *you* get to choose to be a victim or a victor? *Re-new your mind!*

- We subject ourselves to consistent setbacks when we insist on revisiting a past that will never be favorably available to us in our present or our future. We have to be brave enough to let go and walk by faith into an unknown but definite future!

- **It is impossible for God to lie!**

- We have a big enough job controlling our own negative mental chatter. Do not accept outside negativity as your own!

- Repentance must come after sin, so that there is freedom. Turn away, which means to turn around!

- The Bible continues to refer to Bathsheba as "Uriah's wife" even after David married her! Her name does not change until the baby dies *and* after worship and repentance. Who is God calling *us!* —**2 Samuel 12:21–24**

- The Word of God is not a book of illustrations and stories for our entertainment (one of the biggest lies that the enemy wants us to believe), but it is God's gift/instruction manual to us that will guide us through *all* events and circumstances in our lives!

- Change on the outside is just a temporary fixer-upper if it is not rooted from the inside! **Psalms 51:10—Create in me a pure heart, O God, and renew a steadfast spirit within me.**

- When we stand before the judge of the whole earth, we might be shocked to discover how many of our opinions and pontifications were not divinely sanctioned or endorsed even though we claimed them to be so—-Bishop Mark Chironna, Twitter@markchironna, 6/15/2019.

- There will be *no* breakthrough, healing, or deliverance if transparency and honesty is not entrusted with the "Counselor!"

- While we are here today, many of us live in the past and miss what is currently taking place in the present. You can't get today back; so, every day, tell yourself that you will no longer reside in the shadows of what has passed away until every day becomes your present . . . *gift*!

- When you know in whom your power lies and how to access that power and you believe, it is impossible to stay stuck in situations or circumstances that hinder your inheritance.

- Time out for using others as an excuse for the negative condition of our lives. Others may have been perpetrators, but because we have the Holy Spirit, now we are equipped to make changes in our lives, to the glory of God!

- No matter how sad, down, frustrated, upset you are, how he or she has gotten on your very last nerve, how aggravated and angry you are, you can't take it anymore, you're weary or just plain tired, the moment that you turn away and start talking to and praising God, although the circumstances may remain the same, *you* have changed, because you refocused your view and moved closer to God. With God, there is peace on the other side of that mountain!

- As a child, you grew and developed under your parent's history and circumstances; but as an adult, you are able to manipulate your future, not just based on what you have been taught, but based on what you have learned through the assistance of the Holy Spirit!

- ❖ Mary Magdalene did not recognize Jesus at the tomb after his resurrection until He called her name. Most times, it will take the Lord calling our names in order for us to recognize Him in our lives. **John 20:14–16—At this, she turned around and saw Jesus standing here, but she did not realize that it was Jesus. He asked her, "Woman, why are you crying? Who is it you are looking for?" Thinking he was the gardener, she said, "Sir, if you have carried him away, tell me where you have put him, and I will get him." Jesus said to her, "Mary." She turned toward him and cried out in Aramaic, "Rabboni," which means teacher.**

- ❖ **Psalms 34:17—When the righteous cry for help, the Lord hears and delivers them out of all their troubles.**

- ❖ Some things you just can't avoid, so you may have to cry your way through it. But God is always with you as you go through and when you get to the other side!

- ❖ Rest in the fact that God is moving, even though you have no visibility at times!

- ❖ There are some things or people you think you will never get over and then one day, you realize that "sick feeling" is no longer there when you think about it or them. It is behind you; that is called deliverance.

- ❖ We are all going to get upset about things and people, but the important thing to remember is "Do not sin in your anger!" Plenty of times I have had to talk to the Lord with tears running down my face in pain almost the entire time or call someone that I trust in order to keep from sinning! That does not make us awful, but it verifies that we are sinners and saved by grace! Ignoring our pain is like having cancer in one area, and because it is not addressed, it metastasizes. Don't allow anger to become wrath!

- ❖ God will give you spiritual sight again and remove the fabricated leaves used for hiding. **Genesis 3:7—Then the eyes of both were opened, and they knew that they were naked. And they sewed fig leaves together and made themselves loincloths.**

- ❖ A sign of maturity is when you allow Jesus to take you where you don't want to go! —Bishop Mark Chironna, Twitter@markchironna 3/13/2019.

- ❖ Process is where the blessing lies; it secures the integrity and authentication of the blessing.

July's Relationship Reflections

★ Naomi sent Ruth to the threshing floor and gave specific instructions regarding Boaz. Ruth followed her instructions, which included asking Boaz to cover her with his skirt/anointing! It amazes me that God's grace through faith will send you to the place that holds your blessing, which is not just a physical place, but a place of love and obedience! **Ruth 3:1–10.**

★ In relationship building, two people can't afford to read the same book and stay in different chapters. Both must navigate to the same page . . . through desire!

- Know when to hold on to your heart until there is someone worthy to share it with. **Proverbs 4:23—Above all else, guard your heart, for everything you do flows from it.**

- Men and women who are interested in each other should ask questions about one another in an attempt to form a connection because that shows genuine interest. Responses should be respected, even if you don't agree with some of those responses.

- I absolutely love a gentle and sensitive man of God because the backdrop is usually *strength* and *power*! Listen and watch his "tone"!

Notes

August's Aroma

Fear

Isaiah 41:10—Fear not, for I am with you; be not dismayed, for I am your God; I will strengthen you, I will help you, I will uphold you with my righteous right hand.

- ❖ The antidote to fear is to focus on God and His Word. He is always with us.

- ❖ Over this last year, I have learned not to fear obedience to God because where He is taking me as a result of my obedience is better than I could have ever thought or imagined.

- No matter how big they are, how many they are, how persistent they are or how intimidating they sound—-*No weapon formed will prosper!*

  Isaiah 54:17—No weapon that is formed against thee shall prosper; and every tongue that shall rise against thee in judgment thou shalt condemn. This is the heritage of the servants of the LORD, and their righteousness is of me, saith the LORD.

- The next time you are near God's open door, push past fear and walk through it.

   - *Have a great day and trust God!*

- When a child is not given space or room to express what they are feeling or experiencing for fear of rejection, the truth will always mutate into a lie. It works the same way in adults.

- Don't shrink yourself to make other people feel comfortable. It has to be an insult to God! You are fearfully and wonderfully made!

- Being "yourself" may not be popular, but uniqueness has no shelf life! In the midst of the crowd, be who God calls you to be!

- Always needing to be in control, means being out of control! We have to trust God and let go.

- We don't have to allow the fear of love to be our nemesis any longer. Choosing God is choosing love!

- Even with all that we are facing today, never be convinced that pain's representatives (hurt, anger, fear, etc.) are permanent fixtures or conditions in our lives. It is simply an indication that healing exists.

- There may be times that saying to another what is in our hearts may not get us the result that we envision, but it will free us from the boulder of fear!

- Whatever you ask God to do, no worries, He can handle it!

- It is impossible to move to the next season if you have one foot still in the last one. Step out, so that you can walk in!

- We have the God-given ability to make choices or stay on the fence forever. Press past your fear.

- Fear is the "love child" of circumstance and doubt—Bishop David G. Evans, Facebook, 5/14/2020.

- Stop worrying about people not including you in their lives. You are etched in God's hand, not theirs!

- Many times, we are unable to see clearly because of the many veils in our presence. But when trouble stirs up, causing fear to show its face, know that God is just allowing the illumination of our enemies, adversaries, naysayers, as well as our allies, so that our vision can become clear!

- I woke up at 2:05 a.m. this morning with this in my spirit: **Psalm 91:5—You will not fear the terror of night, nor the arrow that flies by day** —*God has us covered!* There have been many times that I have had to read this entire precious Psalm 91 to *remember* and *ask God* to take away fear and restore *peace, faith, and trust* to the forefront of my life while praying for the same blessings in the lives of others!

- Don't be discouraged by roadblocks. Be encouraged: God will either move it or move you. He will keep you on course!

- It will be alright. Sometimes we have to take a "break," so that *it* does not break us! God needs us for the work and the *victory*!

- When you run from fear, it just keeps chasing you ... for years! If you want deliverance from fear, it may be scary and it may *hurt like the hell that birthed it;* but look it in the face, call it a liar and it will flee. God is *not* the author of fear! **2 Timothy 1:7—For God hath not given us the spirit of fear; but of power, and of love, and of a sound mind.**

- Be encouraged, that last season of fear, difficulty, pain, and confusion is over!

- Fear will begin to *disappear* as we stay in the presence of God!

- ❖ Worry, sadness, anxiety, envy, jealousy, depression, heartache, sickness, apathy as well as fear can all be *distractions!*
- ❖ Be fearless, knowing that God has firmly placed His hand on you. Nothing that the enemy attempts will stop God!
- ❖ Adversaries do not penetrate God's connection. It strengthens and seals it!
- ❖ The enemy's mission is to have us *place ourselves* in a state of paralytic fear because he knows that it will move us away from the *mind of God*.
- ❖ Your enemies don't understand why you are still standing, in spite of all of the fiery darts that are thrown at you—-*Nobody but God!*
- ❖ The enemy attempts to use "silence" as a weapon against you, so make sure that in those times of silence, you remember what God already told you!
- ❖ Fear can immobilize us at times, but we must realize that life's circumstances can be bittersweet. Be grateful for both and count it all joy. Celebrate the sweet and learn from the bitter.
- ❖ When we change our focus from the *one* that shackles to the *One* that frees ... then we are free in *Deed*!

August's Relationship Reflections

★ Love will always build up! Real love will never tear down under any circumstances because love can't fail!

★ Women: Make-up or no make-up, weave or no weave, natural, perm or Keratin treatment, color or no color, eyelashes or no eyelashes, nails or no nails, Nordstrom or Walmart, we all have a flavor that stems from our uniqueness in the Almighty God. While He is so gracious to allow us to develop in His beautiful rainbow of choices, it does not come close to *all* of who we are in our relationship with Him! So, as we express our unique flavors on the outside, make sure that we *adorn* ourselves with the

On This Day...

beauty of His word in our hearts and wear it as if our lives depend on it because it does!

★ Young women: If you have to choose between status, money, or good character, pick the latter because that is the building blocks to having great wealth!

★ Take inventory because you do not want to spend a good part of your life with the wrong person or none of your life with the *right person!* Always consult God!

★ Manhood is a journey—Bishop David G. Evans, Facebook, 4/22/2018.

Notes

September's Sessions

Prayer

1 Thessalonians 5:17—Pray without ceasing.

- ❖ Joint pain. When we pray for someone else, God can heal the one we are praying for, and then He searches the one that prays and heals their hidden wounds as well.

- ❖ Every prayer that you pray for an enemy is a good seed that grows in fertile soil!

- ❖ Don't allow the sun to go down without giving our troubles and worries to God!

- ❖ It is better to pray and ask God to reveal His purpose for our lives than to covet someone else's.

- Prayer and Fasting moves you closer to God and synchronizes your hearing!
- The Lord speaks to us way more than we listen to Him. Pray and pay attention!
- People can seem happy, confident, in control, and exhibit what looks like love, but inside they may be suicidal. When God brings someone to your heart... Please pray!
- Sometimes a break is needed from the weight of your life, *so that you can lean on God*. Take it to the *altar*!
- Prayer is one of the most powerful weapons that you will ever have.
- When you get to the point that you can pray and step aside with the Author's faith intact, you will have mastered your present and your future! **Hebrews 12:2—Looking unto Jesus, the author and finisher of our faith; who for the joy that was set before him endured the cross, despising the shame, and is set down at the right hand of the throne of God.**
  - **Today, pray for awakening and revival!**
- When we pray, the Holy Spirit, as our mediator, takes those prayers to the *counsel* (Father, Son, and Holy Spirit) on our behalf. The Bible says that the prayers of the righteous avail much! Calvary has given us the ability to go boldly to the throne of grace and petition the *counsel* through the Holy Spirit to bless and change some stuff in our lives and the lives of those that we are assigned to love.
- Try this for one week and you won't be able to stop. Before you go to bed at night, take a few minutes and think about all the good things that God has done for you that day. Then name them and thank Him, not *loud*, but out loud. Next, thank Him for all the negative things that He kept you from that day; some things you will never know about; not *loud*, but out loud (you are having a conversation). As a result, a few things will happen: You will begin to think of more good things as the week progresses, you will start to actually become more grateful

for His love for you, you will smile more throughout the day, and the best thing of all that will happen, *you will love being in His presence!*

- ❖ It is my prayer that the Words that God gives me to share will bless at least one; if so, then I have served Him well!

- ❖ Every time someone is mean, intentionally hurtful or hateful toward you, that is simply an invitation to pray. Prayer changes things!

- ❖ **Romans 8:26—In the same way, the Spirit helps us in our weakness. We do not know what we ought to pray for, but the Spirit himself intercedes for us through wordless groans.**

- ❖ Father in Heaven, in the mighty name of *Jesus*, I bind *all* attempts that dare come against *your* divine destiny for our lives. Amen.

- ❖ Our greatest up-liftings have come after our lowest points because we yelled "Jesus, help!" and He stretched *His hand out to us*!

- ❖ There are so many people in "need" in places that the naked eye can't see! Open your heart in prayer and ask God to show you theirs. Be a blessing!

- ❖ When you are talking to God in the secret place, there is no level of education or degree necessary! Words will come very easy to you when you have a heart for God, and He will answer.

- ❖ Some of our most profound lessons are learned in secret.

- ❖ Sometimes the best thing to do is tell the Lord that you don't know what to do! Go to the altar!

- ❖ We will never understand "the things of God" unless we allow Him to be our interpreter through the power of the Holy Spirit.

- ❖ Through prayer, you are taking a step back, allowing God to wrap His arms around those you care about. God is a healer and deliverer.

- ❖ Years ago, there was a movie on television called *The Bad Seed*. That movie scared me as a child because the bad seed was a beautiful little blonde girl who had a demonic spirit. As the years passed and through prayer, I learned to bypass a person's appearance and look for the window to their heart by what they said *and* did, over time. A tree is recognized by the fruit that it bears. A bad seed cannot produce good fruit!

- ❖ God knows when to let us "lay our heads on His shoulder . . . through prayer."

- ❖ Pray for marriages and relationships. God can give life or restore any seemingly dead thing.

- ❖ Time to pick up the Word of God and kneel (pray) at His feet!

- ❖ Pray for God's healing power for those that are close to us. They have been broken right along with us!

- ❖ I asked my daughter to pray and ask God to speak through me as I share what he has given me with others, and this is what she wrote: "Mom, I pray for you every day. But I'm going to send something extra special up to God today; He's got you. You're destined for greatness. Now it's time to walk in it. I'm very proud of you, Mom. You're everything. Never forget that. I love you!." Amazing, youth speaking destiny to the elder!

- ❖ Make sure that in your daily prayers you take a moment to lift up your pastors, preachers, ministers, and reverends. All who are called to service by God to shepherd His people. Prayer covers them and their assignment, which includes *all of us*!

September's Relationship Reflections

★ Men: Here is a little secret about us women. The reason that the women in your lives respect, love, and honor you, whether she is your mother, wife, daughter, sister, etc., is because when you speak and keep a word, in her heart—whether she knows this or not—you are reflecting God! He speaks a Word and it is done! He is a promise keeper. All of His promises are yea and amen! So, you don't have to spend every dime on us, say yes to everything that we ask, take us out every night or always give us lavish gifts (although we would like that sometimes!); just be consistent! Be that man of God that keeps his word!

- ★ Relationships are gifts from God. Take your time unwrapping them!

- ★ Never be upset because you are number two in your future husband or wife's lives. As a matter of fact, you shouldn't have it any other way . . . As long as their number one is the Lord God!!

- ★ Sometimes the most contentious individuals seem to connect with the weakest individuals; both want power, but for different reasons!

- ★ Similar strengths give you mutual attraction that isn't just about looks—Bishop David G. Evans, Facebook, 5/3/2018.

Notes

October's Outlook

Doubt, Pain, Obedience, and Offense

James 1:6-8—But when you ask, you must believe and not doubt, because the one who doubts is like a wave of the sea, blown and tossed by the wind. That person should not expect to receive anything from the Lord. Such a person is double-minded and unstable in all they do.

- ❖ Let go of the past pain so that love can enter, trusting that God will send someone to protect the integrity of your heart.

- When the enemy plants vain imaginations in your mind, don't meditate on them. You have the power and authority to cast them down.

  2 Corinthians 10:5—Casting down imaginations, and every high thing that exalteth itself against the knowledge of God, and bringing into captivity every thought to the obedience of Christ.

- There are those that you will never be able to please no matter what you do; they are blinded to you on purpose! Put your energy into pleasing God and many of those that love Him will adore you!

- You will know when you have triumphed over an offense because the next time you see the offender, all that you will have in your heart is peace and a prayer.

- Stop spending precious time hating and co-conspiring hate, which is not a reflection of the object of hate, but one's own poor perception of self. Start *looking up* to the one that has made you in His image and likeness and that translates into *all things beautiful and lovely*!

- When doubt comes, read your Word and do some homicide on it. The Word of God is poison to doubt—Bishop David G. Evans, Facebook, 8/5/2018.

- Never allow anyone or anything to negatively infiltrate the good soil of your heart. Guard your heart against filthy infiltration!

- There is no place in the Kingdom for envy, jealousy, and petty competition. God has gifted each one of us through truth and grace.

- Envy, jealousy, and hatred are all symptoms of *pain*. Evict them now in Jesus' name!

- God will turn the enemy's purpose of the offense around and make it bless you.

- They can't shatter you when you are insulated! Wolves belong on the outside of your house. Guard your heart!

- When we disobey God, we are not just affecting our own life, but we alter the lives of those that are connected to us as well.

- **One positive daily change will create the life that wants to emerge.**

- You are greater, much greater. Eyes have not seen, nor ears heard what God is going to do in your life. That is why the enemy is fighting you with everything he has, but he will lose because *you are greater*. So many more people will be blessed by God because of who you are in Him. Stay focused on God! **1 John 4:4—Ye are of God, little children, and have overcome them: because greater is he that is in you than he that is in the world.**

- Don't allow the Word that God spoke yesterday and you have accepted, to be snatched away today!

- We say it, but do we always believe it? The reason we have overcome is that we are *not* by ourselves. God is with us! Glorify Him for that!

- Some folks carry a welcome mat called "Confusion"! They live it, love it, and attempt to infuse it. Move past it!

- When someone "unintentionally" tells you who they are, it is still your responsibility to believe them. **Matthew 12:34— You brood of vipers, how can you who are evil say anything good? For the mouth speaks what the heart is full of.**

- I know it's not always easy, but we can't resort to mimicking the offender. We are higher.

- People's thoughts and opinions change from day to day, so be very careful who you allow to feed you and on what day they hand it out. *God never changes!*

- Tests, trials, and life's circumstances will *always reveal* adversaries and enemies because they can see your blessed future!

- No one likes it, but it is necessary: pain. Don't run from it. If God brought you to it, then He is taking you through it. Pain will always precede healing and deliverance.

- Hatefulness, meanness, and vindictiveness cannot be hidden. But we can ask God for a clean heart and a right spirit. He will do it for us through the transforming power of *love*!

- There will come a point in your life that you will become so connected to God and what He says about your life and who you are in Him, that the opinions of others—that pass and change as often as this heavy wind that I hear outside right now—will take a back seat, especially if the originator is not God!! Don't flip-flop your life because of what someone thinks or says about you today, that may be different tomorrow. Stand on your connection with God!

- When God gives me a word to write, I have to admit that there are times I don't know why He gave me that particular word. At times, I was a bit fearful about writing what He said because I didn't want to write the wrong thing and I definitely didn't want to hurt anyone, and so I put it off. I admit that I questioned what He was saying! However, I had to learn to be obedient because He knows what I don't. So, I resumed while attempting to be as encouraging as I could! Amazingly, when I go back and read over what I wrote previously, I find that there was *always* a lesson for me that I never saw when I first wrote it. God will teach us first! Be obedient to God's leadings, it is better than sacrifice!

- Maturity means owning and then learning from our mistakes. Will we have liberty or not?

- If God spoke yesterday, but is silent today, it is because *He has not changed His mind!*

- Many have the tendency to romanticize what is distant. But are we able to stay in the trenches when the fantasy becomes reality?

- Ironically, many times when people attempt to label you and place you in a box, it has nothing to do with you. It has more to do with where the confines of their minds feel most comfortable visiting you. So, when their breakthrough happens, it has little to do with you and everything to do with their deliverance. They were in the box, not *you*.

- ❖ Emotions are feelings compiled from our backgrounds, knowledge, moods, etc. They are designed to help us manage our lives and help move us toward a desired direction. However, the operative word is "manage." We should not be led by our emotions. They are tools given to us by God. When the management of our emotions becomes unbalanced, these same tools can then become internal weapons. Emotions are managed by staying close to God in prayer and His word for constant renewal and strength. **Proverbs 25:28—A man without self-control is like a city broken into and left without walls.**

- ❖ Mistreatment, betrayal, heartbreak, death, lies, and cheating are just the "sandpaper" God allows to make you shine!

- ❖ Many of us are guilty of this to some degree and we must do better: We can see clearly someone else's faults, but seem to miss the beam in our own eyes! Stay humble; it's convicting.

October's Relationship Reflections

- ★ In the scripture below, God had not yet taken the rib out of Adam to form Eve; however, she was still present! Your connection may not be manifested yet, but they are present, waiting to be revealed. **Genesis 1:27—So God created mankind in his own image, in the image of God he created them; male and female he created them.**

- ★ Predictability produces security—Bishop David G. Evans, Twitter@davidgevans1, 5/2/2018.

- ★ A man or woman of God is not manipulative, intrusive, combative, or hurtful, and definitely not hateful toward his or her love interest, simply because he or she knows and loves God first. And so, the fruit of their first love will be evidenced in their relationship.

★ A man or woman who preys on your weaknesses under the guise of "love" should not be the one you're longing for. However, a man or woman who lifts you when you are weak, vulnerable, and even broken, is the one you should seek and recognize! Ask God to give you eyes to see again! Men—Stay away from Delilah! Women—Strengthen Samson!

★ Ladies, the right man will approach you with care and thought; you've been on his mind!

Notes

November's Nuggets

Encouragement

Romans 8:31—What then shall we say to these things? If God is for us, who can be against us?

- ❖ Don't wait for anyone; encourage yourself today.
- ❖ We all love the virtuous woman of Proverbs 31. She is phenomenal. It's certainly an attainable goal, simply because "it is written."

  Proverbs 31: 10–31

  A wife of noble character, who can find? She is worth far more than rubies. Her husband has full confidence in her and lacks nothing of value. She brings him good, not harm, all the days of her life. She

selects wool and flax and works with eager hands. She is like the merchant ships, bringing her food from afar. She gets up while it is still night; she provides food for her family and portions for her female servants. She considers a field and buys it; out of her earnings, she plants a vineyard. She sets about her work vigorously; her arms are strong for her tasks. She sees that her trading is profitable, and her lamp does not go out at night. In her hand, she holds the distaff and grasps the spindle with her fingers. She opens her arms to the poor and extends her hands to the needy. When it snows, she has no fear for her household; for all of them are clothed in scarlet. She makes coverings for her bed; she is clothed in fine linen and purple. Her husband is respected at the city gate, where he takes his seat among the elders of the land. She makes linen garments and sells them and supplies the merchants with sashes. She is clothed with strength and dignity; she can laugh at the days to come.

She speaks with wisdom, and faithful instruction is on her tongue. She watches over the affairs of her household and does not eat the bread of idleness. Her children arise and call her blessed; her husband also, and he praises her: "Many women do noble things, but you surpass them all." Charm is deceptive, and beauty is fleeting, but a woman who fears the LORD is to be praised. Honor her for all that her hands have done and let her works bring her praise at the city gate.

- ❖ Make a habit of speaking words of encouragement into the lives of those that God has blessed you to touch!
- ❖ Your destiny is never just for you; you have connections!

Encouragement

- ❖ Did you know that there is *no ceiling* in a child's imagination? They can reach as high as their imagination will take them, and all we have to do is go along for the ride through *encouragement*!

- ❖ You are fearfully and wonderfully made just like Sarah, Rebecca, Job, and Joseph because of the greatness of God. There is no need for comparison.

- ❖ Every chance that you get, speak positively over your children's and grandchildren's lives and make sure that they hear you speak it. Even if they haven't exhibited their potential yet, it's OK. Keep speaking, until promise comes to pass!

- ❖ **Believe God all day long!**

- ❖ Sometimes God needs to pull things from our past and bring it to the forefront to remind us of what He has already done for us!

- ❖ Teach your daughters and sons who they are in God through the Word of God, at an early age!

- ❖ There will be times that the "package" in which God presents someone may not look like what you *envisioned* for yourself, but just hold on while God finishes the unwrapping. This one is for you!

- ❖ No matter how gifted or blessed another individual is, no other human being can make a change in your life, but *you*!

- ❖ Some think that appearing to be "perfect" is evidence of being close to God when our *imperfections* are what attracts Him to us! When we are weak, He is strong!

- ❖ God keeps giving us chance after chance until our life matches the finished portrait that He painted for us . . . in the beginning!

- Your position with man is never etched in stone; it changes continually. But your life is engraved in the palm of God's hand.

  Isaiah 49:16—See, I have engraved you on the palms of my hands; your walls are ever before me.

- Hireling or shepherd?

  It matters where you go to church—-Bishop David G. Evans, sermon 12/1/2013

- A balloon will burst if too much air enters, a rubber band stretched past its limit will break, and a tea kettle will start to blow with steam escaping when water begins to bubble and boil. While we are not inanimate objects, we will be taxed over our limits at times. So, be grateful that we can go to God so that some air will be let out of that balloon, the rubber band will be relaxed, and the tea kettle will be *removed from the fire!* He allows what we can't handle so that we give it to Him. The stressful situation may be the same, but our perspective shifts by giving the excess weight over to the weight-bearer!

- While focusing on the thing(s) that are not quite correct for our lives, our periphery is still there! It was always there. The blessings were always in the periphery, waiting to be seen. Process brings correct things into focus!

- Process to purpose to destiny. God protects it for you; you discover it. It's yours to grow and thrive in. It's a treasure hunt!

- Keep asking, seeking, and knocking until your expectations and desires become God's preferred will for your life!

- There is a special blessing waiting when we do for others that which we need done for ourselves.

- Birthing anything great is painful, but oh, so worth it!

- Rebirth and new beginnings do not always mean that you have to pack up and leave, but it does mean that you have to be born again. A renewal of the heart and mind has to take place. Same place, same people, clean heart, right spirit.

Encouragement

- Always ask God for "eyes to see" so that you never disregard, ignore, overlook, or throw away the blessings that He has fashioned just for you!

- When seeds are sown into the ground, they are no longer visible until they begin to take root, so that what was hidden in the seeds become visible above ground. *Sow your seed!*

- Your brain is your garden. God is your gardener. Seed is God's word. Seed planted in your garden by the gardener changes the mind—-Bishop David G. Evan, Twitter@davidgevans1, 2/28/2019.

- To many, it may look like the promotion came from "them," but promotion comes from God. **Psalm 75:6–7—For promotion cometh neither from the east, nor from the west, nor the south. But God is the judge; he putteth down one, and setteth up another.**

- Do exactly what God says, when He says it, because slow to obedience is still disobedience, and it *delays His will for your life.*

- When a womb is closed (a place of incubation), nothing can grow. But God opens wombs with no regard to time. He did it for Sarah, Rebecca, Hanna, and He *can* do it for *you* . . . If you believe!

- Dashboard windows are huge compared to rearview mirrors for a reason. Your focus has to be in front of you as you move forward while checking periodically to see what is behind you so your course forward stays smooth. If someone behind you is coming fast, you can change lanes to get out of their way. It may be your past trying to catch up with you . . . *again*!

- **3 John 1:2—Beloved, I wish that above all things that thou mayest prosper and be in health, even as thy soul prospereth.**

November's Relationship Reflections

★ Pay attention to how the man or woman that you are interested in treats those who they believe can't advance them in any way.

★ Satan has a plan for your "boo." You can't help him physically fight it. It's a one-on-one fight within every man—Bishop David G. Evans, Facebook, 4/22/2018.

★ "Be cautious of the man or woman who just wants an easy person. The person who is not going to force them to grow, who is not going to expect them to change, who is not going to hold them accountable. You would not pick someone off the bench who is going to show up weak. You want to pick somebody who is going to carry you through. Those are the things that get you over the hard times," the mother of two said. —Michele Obama, Briefly.co.za, 11/25/2019.

★ It would be great to make a connection and never have an issue or a problem, but that is not life's reality. However, it is possible to have a successful and loving relationship when God is the center vessel in a three-vessel cord!

★ The one that you are praying for will come into your life when you relinquish *all* to God! Let Him guide him or her to you. His grace is sufficient!

Notes

December's Discussions

Trust

Psalms 37:5—Commit your way to the LORD; trust in him, and he will act.

- ❖ There are really no words to describe God; but He is a waymaker, a deliverer, comforter, revealer, promise keeper, bridge over troubled waters, storm chaser, prayer answerer, trusted friend, healer, etc. There is no one greater than God!

- ❖ There is overflow in the Kingdom of God. There is more than enough for all of us to be blessed. You need restoration; you want a business, a husband, a wife, healing, and deliverance, etc., God will provide. *He is more than enough!*

- ❖ We speak positive words into our future, but do we really believe or are we just running a recorder of empty words with no faith base! Hear, speak, believe . . . then trust!
- ❖ We must be like the woman who has overcome the issue of blood! Jesus' virtue must be transferred to us! Trust that God will make us whole while moving us closer toward our destiny in Him!

Luke 8:43–48

And a woman was there who had been subject to bleeding for twelve years, but no one could heal her. She came up behind him and touched the edge of his cloak, and immediately her bleeding stopped. "Who touched me?" Jesus asked.

When they all denied it, Peter said, "Master, the people are crowding and pressing against you." But Jesus said, "Someone touched me; I know that power has gone out from me." Then the woman, seeing that she could not go unnoticed, came trembling and fell at his feet. In the presence of all the people, she told why she had touched him and how she had been instantly healed. Then he said to her, "Daughter, your faith has healed you. Go in peace."

- ❖ Trusting God facilitates your ability to trust again. Do it through Him!
- ❖ Always allow God to move you.
- ❖ There are some doors that God steps in with you and closes! We are *locked in* for His purpose for our lives!
- ❖ When we finally learn to hear, see, and trust God *through* His vessels, we will take down podiums and stages for people and build altars for Him!
- ❖ When God blesses you, it may also be a seed to bless someone else. Don't be afraid to release it. Seeds regenerate!

- Whatever good and positive thought that crosses your mind, hijack and claim It. That is God speaking to you!
- When God shuts a door that you can't enter... Trust Him. It is on purpose!
  - **This week, no matter what presents itself...believe God.**
- If God reveals to His chosen apostles and prophets "in part," then how can those, without seeking Him, think that they see all. **Leviticus 19:31—Do not turn to mediums or necromancers; do not seek them out, and so make yourselves unclean by them: I am the LORD your God.**
- I took a walk in the rain; it was exhilarating! I admit that there were a few things that I was not happy about, *but* I actually caught myself smiling as I was walking and thanking God that I am healthy enough to *walk*! I realized that it is the joy of the Lord that keeps me! Let's be grateful even in the midst of trouble. Even if the trouble stays for a while, that is A-OK because we have *Joy*!
- Over time, life's tests, trials, and circumstances can cause you to lose your voice. Fight to get it back; God gave it to you!
- When it seems dark, trust God. He does some of His best work in the midnight hour!
- The enemy is like a professional thief who sneaks up behind you, on your side, or even in front of you, and without you even realizing it, every good thing is gone! **James 4:7—Submit yourselves, then, to God. Resist the devil, and he will flee from you.**
- The things of God are revealed by the Spirit.
- **John 15:5—I am the vine; you are the branches. If you remain in me and I in you, you will bear much fruit; apart from me, you can do nothing.**
- The future will reveal the reason for the "No," so for now, trust God!

- The Word of God gives us instructions and the Holy Spirit teaches the instructions through the process. Many times, we hear God's instructions but abandon the process. We have all failed tests! But God, through His grace and mercy (lots of retests), we learn that obedience brings favor and purpose. Go with God through the process!

- **Isaiah 43:2—When you pass through the waters, I will be with you; and when you pass through the rivers, they will not sweep over you. When you walk through the fire, you will not be burned; the flames will not set you ablaze.**

- You may think that you are going in one direction and then God gives you a new vision. Trust God because what you thought was a change, was his plan for you the entire time!

- The enemy's playground is always "in the meantime" because you have to pass through it to get to destiny. Refuse his play dates and keep moving toward destiny!

- After years of entertaining disappointment and hurt, we can wake up one morning and realize that a "trust issue" has moved in!

- Real talk: When I get upset and discouraged about that one thing that seems to continuously challenge me (we all have at least one), I have to force myself to start a conversation with God. Yes, with that special issue I have to deliberately turn to God at a time when I just want to cry and hide my head under the covers!

  As my voice crackles, I begin to give Him praise right there in the midst of my pain. I thank Him for never leaving me or forsaking me as the volume and intensity of my voice increases, and I tell Him how wonderful He is and thank Him for guiding my steps. I remember and thank Him for holding on to me the last time that I had to come to Him like this. I glorify Him for the good thing or person that He already sent from the beginning and guess what, the tears stop, courage peeks out of hiding, and I feel myself smiling. Then, a peace that passes understanding begins to cover me like a blanket. So, the next time you are going through something that needs renewed faith and trust, try it . . . *It works!*

- ❖ Don't be in such a hurry that you move ahead of God and out of the proximity of your blessing! *Faith* and *trust* remove hurriedness and anxiety out of the way and replaces them with *peace and patience*!

  Luke 12:27–28—Consider the lilies how they grow: they toil not, they spin not; and yet I say unto you, that Solomon in all his glory was not arrayed like one of these. If then God so clothe the grass, which is today in the field, and tomorrow is cast into the oven; how much more will he clothe you, O ye of little faith?

- ❖ When we study God's word, we will begin to see ourselves in the pages of the Book. For every issue and problem that we can ever face . . . there is an answer for us in *His Word*!

- ❖ Pray for those who may be waiting for you to fall. Just keep trusting God because if you do fall, it will be right into His protective arms!

- ❖ When you trust and believe God, He will protect you from *all* dangers . . . seen and unseen!

- ❖ I just prayed for us. **Matt 7:7, 21:22, Luke 11:9, John 14:14** . . . All of these scriptures are congruent. All promises of God are yes and amen. He is waiting for you to *simply ask and believe!*

- ❖ When we trust God, the effect of any disappointment is grace-filled because we know that He has us covered. **2 Corinthians 12:9—But he said to me, "My grace is sufficient for you, for my power is made perfect in weakness." Therefore, I will boast all the more gladly about my weaknesses, so that Christ's power may rest on me.**

December's Relationship Reflections

★ If the honor is seasonal, the love will be seasonal—-Bishop David G. Evans, Facebook, 4/19/2018.

★ Men and women of God can have impromptu conversations and the Words flow together as if it had been perfectly planned! It's like when rivers and streams flow together and connect with an ocean (*not collide*) and become one body. That is the power of connection through the mediator, The Holy Spirit!

★ When you attempt to "make someone fit" in your life, it's the equivalent of wearing a pair of shoes that are a size too small. They look good on the outside, but you can't function properly because they hurt. I've worn a few pairs that didn't fit. But when you are in the presence, of the right one, nothing will hinder the fit! As a matter of fact, the difficulty and trouble that will come in the right connection for your life will be far *less* felt because God shields, covers, and enhances while allowing the discomfort and pain to aid in you both growing together!

★ Just because they are the first person whom you think about when you wake up, does not mean they are your soulmate! Many wake up with someone on their heart and that someone wakes up with another on their heart and then the other holds someone else in their heart! Eros with no Philo and no Agape is *out of order!* Guard your *heart*!

★ God asked Samuel, "How long will you mourn over Saul?" Stop crying over who God has already moved out of your life. He has already chosen *another*!

★ Men need demonstrated respect. Women need demonstrated love. Respect feels like love to him. Love feels like respect to her—-Bishop David G. Evans, Facebook, 4/24/2013. **Ephesians 5:33— However, let each one of you love his wife as himself, and let the wife see that she respects her husband.**

★ When the expectations of your connection arrive this time, don't repeat the same negative responses and reactions from your past! If they worked well then, they would not be in the past now.

Notes

CPSIA information can be obtained
at www.ICGtesting.com
Printed in the USA
LVHW050752090920
665328LV00008B/353